By Marielle Munchhaussen
Illustrated by Gabriel Pacheco

Target Skill Draw Conclusions

Brad can not catch the ball.

It goes right on by him.

Where did the ball go, Brad?

Lill can not catch the ball.

She looks at that blue bike!

Where did the ball go, Lill?

3

Stan can not catch that ball.

It goes over his head!

Where did the ball go, Stan?

Tim can not catch the ball.

He looks at the cat!

Where did the ball go, Tim?

Mom will get the cat.

Mom will get the ball.

Where did it go?

Dad will not catch the ball.

He smells a snack to munch!

Where is the ball, Dad?

Gram has snacks to munch.

Gram can catch the ball.

Good catch, Gram!